FAVORITE JAZZ

FOR PIANO SOLO
INTERMEDIATE TO ADVANCED

Arranged by TOM ROED

T0015907

CONTENTS

AIN'T MISBEHAVIN' 15
DON'T GET AROUND MUCH ANYMORE 18
GEORGIA ON MY MIND 20
KILLING ME SOFTLY WITH HIS SONG 32
LINUS AND LUCY 6
MOOD INDIGO 40
ON GREEN DOLPHIN STREET 23
OVER THE RAINBOW 34
RIBBON IN THE SKY 26
THE SHADOW OF YOUR SMILE 45
TAKE FIVE 2
TAKING A CHANCE ON LOVE 29
THE WINDMILLS OF YOUR MIND 42
YOU ARE THE SUNSHINE OF MY LIFE 12
YOU STEPPED OUT OF A DREAM 37

Illustration: Ed Scarisbrick
Copyright © 1990 by the Image Bank
Editor: Tom Roed

© 1994 ALFRED PUBLISHING CO., INC.
All Rights Reserved

TAKE FIVE

By
PAUL DESMOND

Take Five - 4 - 1

4

LINUS AND LUCY

By VINCE GUARALDI

Linus And Lucy - 6 - 1

8

Linus And Lucy - 6 - 4

Linus And Lucy - 6 - 6

YOU ARE THE SUNSHINE OF MY LIFE

By STEVIE WONDER

You Are The Sunshine Of My Life - 3 - 1

From The Broadway Musical Production "AIN'T MISBEHAVIN'"

AIN'T MISBEHAVIN'

By
ANDY RAZAF, THOMAS "FATS" WALLER
and HARRY BROOKS

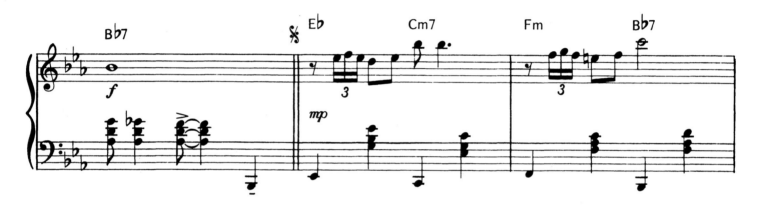

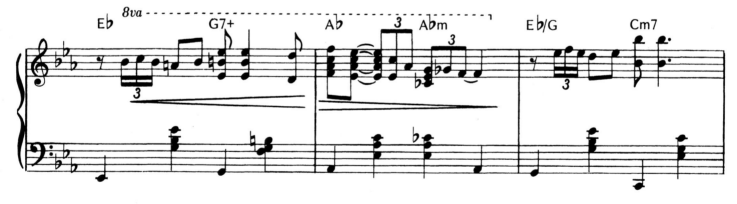

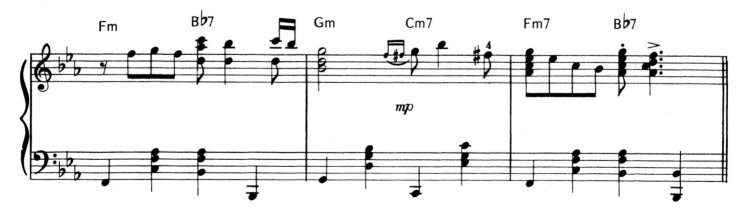

Ain't Misbehavin' - 3 - 1

16

Ain't Misbehavin' - 3 - 3

DON'T GET AROUND MUCH ANYMORE

By
BOB RUSSELL and
DUKE ELLINGTON

Don't Get Around Much Anymore - 2 - 1

Don't Get Around Much Anymore - 2 - 2

GEORGIA ON MY MIND

By
HOAGY CARMICHAEL and
STUART GORRELL

Georgia On My Mind - 3 - 1

Georgia On My Mind - 3 - 2

ON GREEN DOLPHIN STREET

By
NED WASHINGTON and
BRONISLAU KAPER

On Green Dolphin Street - 3 - 1

24

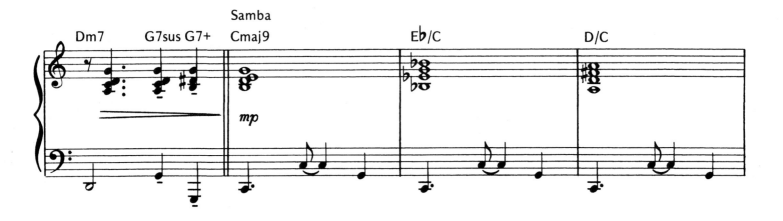

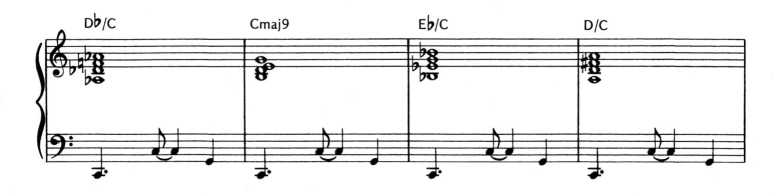

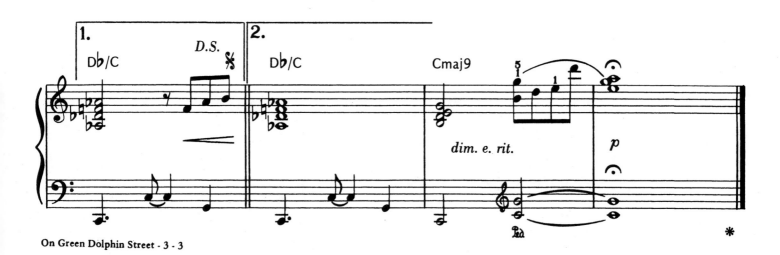

On Green Dolphin Street - 3 - 3

RIBBON IN THE SKY

By
STEVIE WONDER

Ribbon In The Sky - 3 - 1

Ribbon In The Sky - 3 - 2

28

Ribbon In The Sky - 3 - 3

From The M-G-M Musical Production "CABIN IN THE SKY"

TAKING A CHANCE ON LOVE

By
JOHN LATOUCHE, TED FETTER
and VERNON DUKE

Taking A Chance On Love - 3 - 1

Taking A Chance On Love - 3 - 3

KILLING ME SOFTLY WITH HIS SONG

By
NORMAN GIMBEL and
CHARLES FOX

Moderately, flowing ♩ = 108

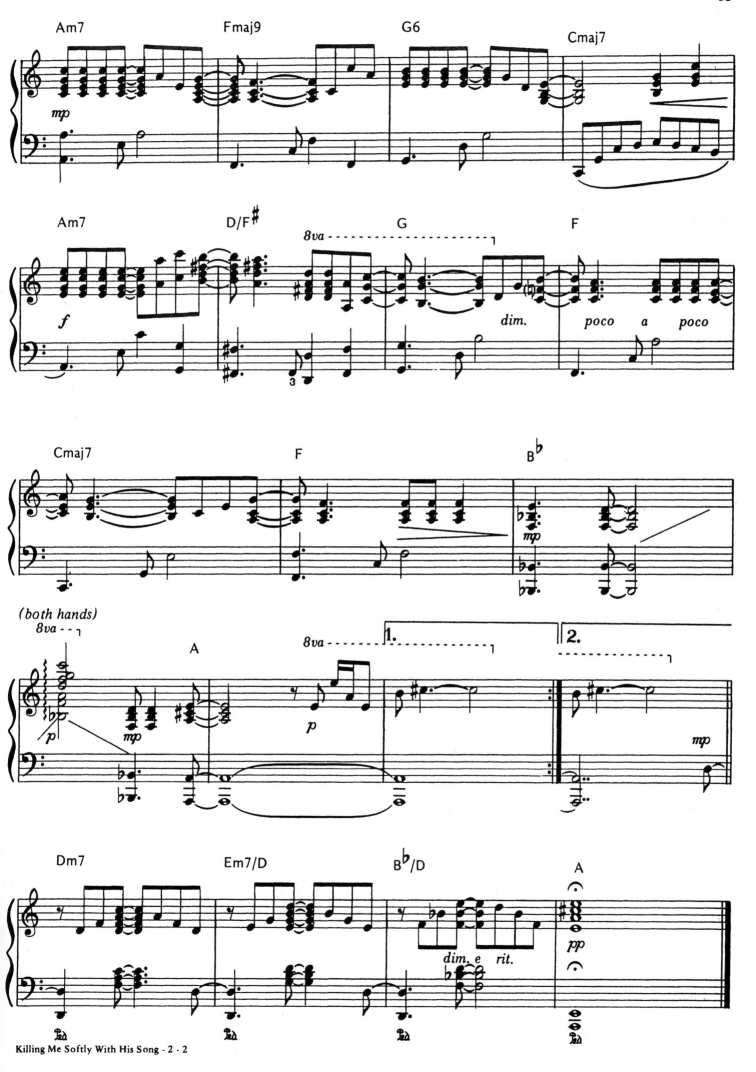

From The Metro-Goldwyn-Mayer Musical Production "THE WIZARD OF OZ"

OVER THE RAINBOW

By
E. Y. HARBURG and
HAROLD ARLEN

Moderately Slow and Expressively ♩ = 84

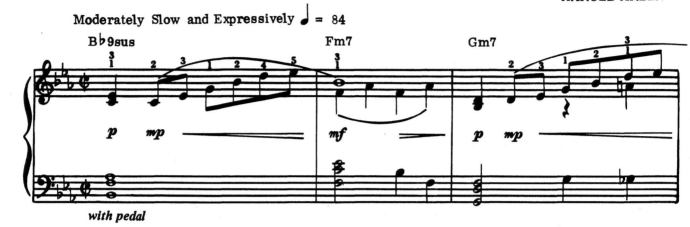

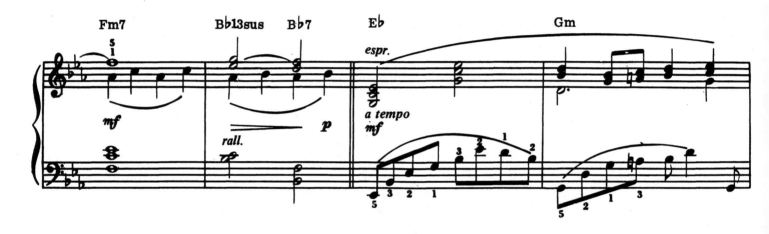

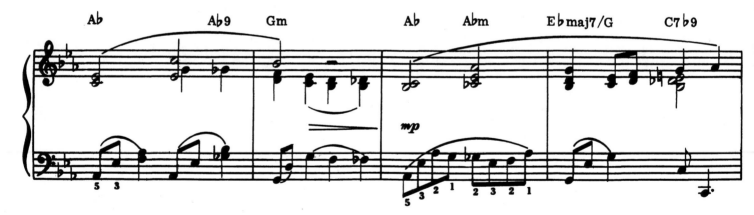

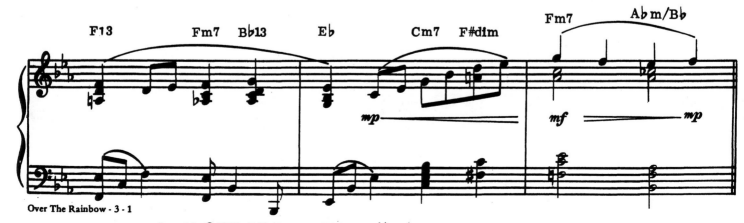

Over The Rainbow - 3 - 1

35

Over The Rainbow - 3 - 2

Over The Rainbow - 3 - 3

From The Metro-Goldwyn-Mayer Musical Production "ZIEGFELD GIRL"

YOU STEPPED OUT OF A DREAM

By
GUS KAHN and
NACIO HERB BROWN

You Stepped Out Of A Dream - 3 - 1

You Stepped Out Of A Dream - 3 - 3

MOOD INDIGO

By
DUKE ELLINGTON, IRVING MILLS
and ALBANY BIGARD

Mood Indigo- 2 - 1

From The United Artists Motion Picture "THE THOMAS CROWN AFFAIR"
Academy Award Winner

THE WINDMILLS OF YOUR MIND

By
MARILYN and **ALAN BERGMAN**
and **MICHEL LEGRAND**

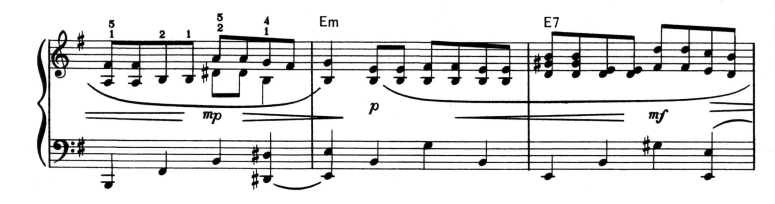

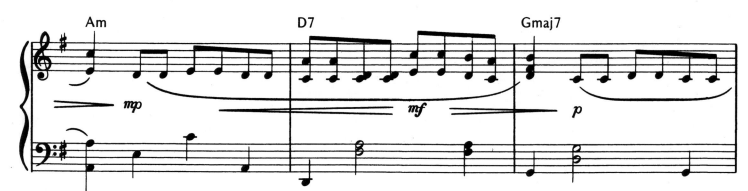

The Windmills Of Your Mind - 3 - 1

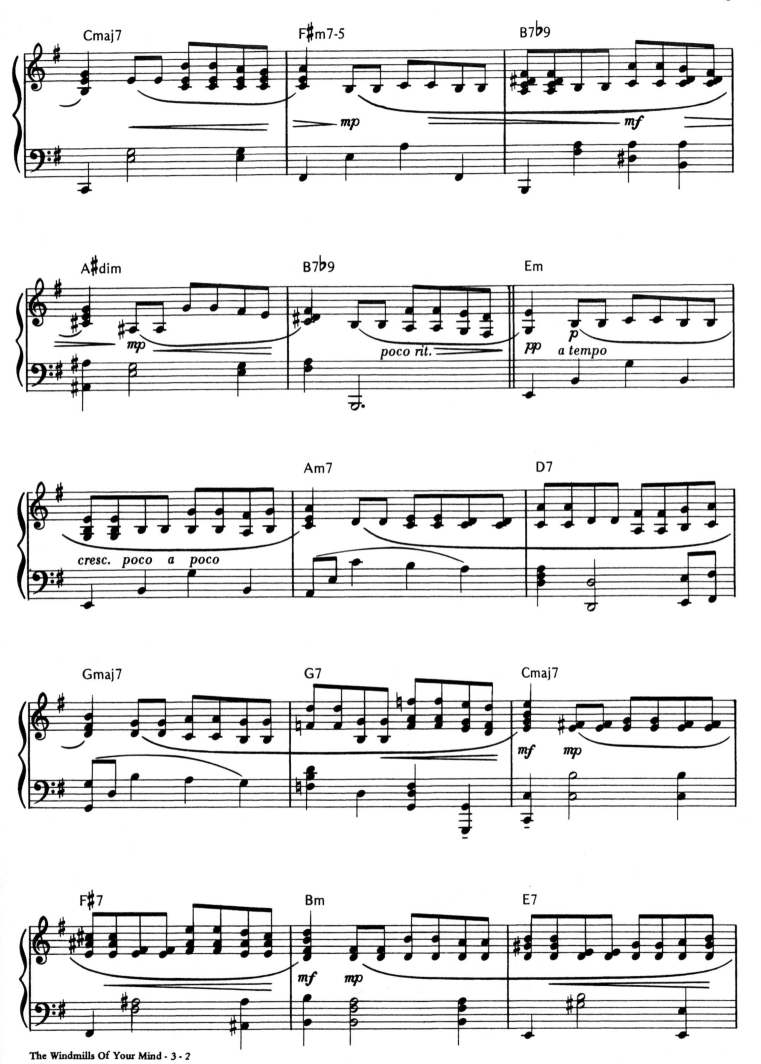

The Windmills Of Your Mind - 3 - 2

The Windmills Of Your Mind - 3 - 3

From The 20th Century-Fox Motion Picture "THE SANDPIPER"

THE SHADOW OF YOUR SMILE

By
PAUL FRANCIS WEBSTER
and JOHNNY MANDEL

The Shadow Of Your Smile - 3 - 1

46

The Shadow Of Your Smile - 3 - 3